I'm getting married
& have NOTHING to wear!

The ultimate guide to finding your
perfect wedding dress!

Nayri Kalayjian

Published by Nayri Kalayjian

Edits by Jennifer M. Barry
Book Cover Design by Becky Rickett, Big Star Production Group
Photo by Simpson Portraits
Bouquet/Florals by Los Angeles Floral Couture by Glendora Florist
Make up by Gabbi Pascua

ISBN: 1987732626
ISBN-13: 978-1987732627

Dedication

This book was inspired by the thousands of brides I have personally assisted through the process of searching for the perfect wedding dress. Soon after getting engaged, every bride faces the same challenge: "OMG, I am getting married and have nothing to wear!"

Your wedding dress is the most important article of clothing you will ever wear. Shopping for your bridal gown isn't like shopping for a new pair of jeans or a cocktail dress. When it comes to everyday wear, you know what works and what doesn't.

Shopping for your bridal gown is a completely different experience. This is why you need a bridal expert to help you evolve in making this decision and guide you through this process.

I'm here to help you with that!

This book is dedicated to my past, present, and future brides: I'm blessed to be a part of this journey with you. Thank you for being my inspiration!

Table of Contents

Introduction

Growing up, I adored all things fashion. Playing dress up was my favorite activity! I envisioned myself being a buyer for a department store, until I had the opportunity to dress my first bride. The importance and excitement of the bond I created with her—and every bride since—was so fulfilling. Having the ability to impact the lives of so many women on a daily basis through fashion feeds my soul!

Naturally, weddings are an important part of my life, or I wouldn't do what I do. Before you trust me with this monumental task, you'll probably want to know more about me. Born and raised in Los Angeles, CA, I grew up in the world of high fashion bridal industry. Given some unique opportunities, I developed a keen eye and distinctive palate at a young age and successfully styled my first bride at age fourteen.

Upon graduating from University of California Santa Barbara, majoring in Sociology, I decided that the bridal industry was my calling in life and the perfect platform to fully engage in the diversity of fashion. More importantly, I chose a platform in which I could support and uplift women in feeling the most confident and beautiful on the most important day in their life: their wedding day!

I've worked hard to refine and fulfill my passion of transforming bride's dreams into reality, creating and styling them and their entire wedding party. I've been featured on various wedding specials styling celebrities as an expert in wedding fashion.

No matter the diverse experiences I've had throughout my career, the same holds true for each wedding dress shopper: with the thrill, comes the overwhelm. I wrote this book based on the most-asked questions and dilemmas I encounter daily at Lovella Bridal and the industry as a whole. This guide provides a wealth of information, clarity, and direction on how to shop and find the perfect wedding dress with ease and enjoyment!

Ready to get started?

Chapter One

Why do I need an expert's help? I know what looks good on my body...

Because we live in a world where we can find answers to anything on the World Wide Web, we often don't seek an expert unless we are in dire need.

For example, my French bulldog Nuff (full name, Sir Nuffington Barnaby) once got his paws on a hair tie that I had set down on my couch. He thought it was a treasure!

His excitement and energy when he got ahold of it was beyond adorable. Something so simple made him the happiest little guy on earth.

I looked at my phone for one second, and when I turned back around to him, the hair tie was gone! He had swallowed it.

I immediately panicked and went straight to Google. Not to the vet. Google. I typed in "How to make a dog throw up?"

Instead of following my first instinct, which was to call the vet who is an expert in this department, I went straight to Google. We all know if you look up anything medically related it all leads to death. I was terrified by all the possible outcomes.

After searching for about five minutes, I looked for local emergency pet hospitals. Their customer service and knowledge was incredible. The vet took him in right away to induce vomiting, and I got the hair tie as a souvenir. Yay, me!

The moral of the story is that we always try to solve problems on our own before seeing an expert. Experts cost money, right?

We can't expect to know how to shop for a bridal gown when we've never done it before. More importantly, just looking at gowns on the rack and expecting to know what they look like on a body is unrealistic. You need an expert who has seen the gown on to guide you and help determine if this is the look you are trying to achieve.

So much of the information found online can be misleading, unless you go straight to the source. A reliable source, of course.

When it comes to your bridal gown, it is so much more than an article of clothing. It is the gown you will begin a new chapter of your life in. It is a gown you'll never forget. Photos will be shown for generations to come.

The beauty of working with a wedding fashion expert stylist is that they know their inventory and what it looks like on different bodies, shapes, and silhouettes.

It's important for you, as the bride, to identify what you like and dislike in your gown, but the stylists' expertise is to present options that you haven't even considered yet.

Many brides who come into Lovella Bridal just let me do my thing. I ask all the questions and get the answers I need to do my job. After that, the magic begins, and they are floored.

Other times, I have clients who don't understand the process because they've never had a complete stranger help them shop for a dress.

These ladies think, "How can this person possibly think they know me and understand what I want to wear on my wedding day?"

When I see that is the frame of mind I'm working with, I take a step back and let them pick three dresses to try on. They can pick whatever they want.

When they are done and more accepting of my input, I provide my choices. In most cases, they love everything I chose and nothing they picked. That's when they finally begin to understand the process.

That is magic! I love to witness that.

On the other hand, I've also had brides come in for a particular dress that they saw we carry. Without much fuss or trying on or decisions agonized over, and they simply buy what they've wanted for a while. So, not every experience is the same.

Every individual has their own needs. You may not like your stylist or have any chemistry with them. That does not mean the store isn't a good fit for you.

Ask for another appointment and to work with someone else. I've had many brides ask to work with someone younger or older than myself.

As stylists and professionals, we do not get offended by this. If you aren't feeling a connection, there is a good chance the stylist didn't feel one either. And that's okay! If you don't express your needs, it's difficult for people to serve you.

To make the very best and most use of your time with a stylist, you can follow these tips:

- Be open, honest, and transparent.
- Express your wants and needs and if you don't know them - express that.
- Take indecision out of the equation (You made a decision on who you will marry. The hardest decision is done! Deciding the dress is a lot like dating; you'll speed date dresses until you find the right fit).
- More failure is caused by indecision than making a choice. Many brides I work with

take pride in being indecisive without realizing that it's a block in making the decision.
- Follow your instinct and don't second guess yourself!

Most importantly, have fun and enjoy!

Chapter Two

What gowns are best for my body shape?

Bridal magazines, experts, and blogs love to provide what shapes look best on certain body types. They usually say something like, "If you have a pear-shaped body you should wear XYZ silhouettes."

The truth is, there is not a dictionary definition or standard protocol when it comes to picking silhouettes for your body. Part of the equation is what you like on your body. The other is what makes you feel beautiful and like the bride you want to be on your wedding day.

Designers these days don't even focus on the dictionary definitions of shapes and silhouettes for gowns. I like to call many gowns hybrids because sometimes designers create a cross between two different dictionary definitions of silhouettes, which leaves the design with no title.

As a bride, don't get hung up on studying the language of all this. Keep things simple for yourself. You need to decide if you want a gown that shows off your body or not.

Try all the shapes on until you find a shape that you like on your body. This is why you also have an expert to help guide you to the dresses that look best on your body so you'll have the look and feel you want for your big day.

You can do all the research you want, but what will determine what you like is actually trying things on.

So, book your appointment and start trying!

Chapter Three

How long does it take to order a dress and what should I know about the selection process?

You should consult with your local bridal store regarding your designer of choice on their current ship dates and lead time, as they are ever changing. However, as a safe rule of thumb wedding dresses typically take six to eight months, on average, to special order. You will want to allow approximately two months for alterations. Again, you must check with your local store to learn their process. A good bet is to plan to purchase your gown about nine months to a year before your wedding, at the bare minimum.

If you're reading this guide and have less than a year until your wedding, do not panic! There are always options. Some designers deliver gowns before the six-to-eight-month mark, and rush orders may also be available for an additional fee.

Another great option for brides with shorter timelines is to consider a sample gown for immediate wear. Just be aware of sample size gowns: If too big or too small, you may need to literally remake the gown during alterations to fit you. We will get into this in greater detail later.

For the brides out there who are overachievers and start the gown shopping process a year and a half or more in advance—which is awesome— keep in mind: If you find something you love, buy it!

I have worked with so many brides who began their search early and thought they had time to wait on purchasing the gown. When they came back months later to purchase, the designer had discontinued the dress, and it was no longer available for purchase.

Another thing to consider is that bridal stores often work with brides who need a dress quickly. Sometimes these stores are forced to sell their sample dress because the bride doesn't have enough time to order. Gowns also get borrowed for photo shoots and may be out of the store for the day.

If you plan to bring guests back to see a particular dress you fell in love with, be sure to call the bridal store a day before or the day of the appointment to make sure they still have it in stock.

Be proactive and make sure your chosen dress is still available. If you take too long to make your decision on a particular dress, you risk having to start your search over again because the gown is no longer available for purchase.

Even brand new designs can get discontinued at any time for various reasons, such as the lace is no longer available, the factory that produced the lace is no longer manufacturing, supply of materials, defects in production and many more.

You must also be mindful of potential price increases. The costs of labor and materials are always going up, and manufacturers and stores do not have control over this.

To sum it up: If you see something you love, go with it. More failure in life is caused by indecision than just making a choice and going for it. Follow your instinct. I can't tell you how many brides show up to sample sales, find the exact dress they want at the perfect price, and walk away from it, all because a loved one or they themselves talked their way out of the purchase. When they return later because they realized walking away was a poor decision, the gown is gone.

When you decide to pass on a tremendous opportunity, ask yourself, "Will I sleep better tonight knowing that I made the right decision to purchase, or will I sleep better knowing I walked away and the next day get into search mode all over again?"

I usually lose sleep when I am indecisive and unable to make a decision, especially when I know the choice I want to make but people around me tell me what they think I should do. Don't let others' indecision lead you to make the wrong choice. Once I make a choice, I can sleep better and am willing to deal with the consequences after the fact, whatever they may be. I encourage you to try this and see if it works for you.

Buying your bridal gown is a little like buying a car. You have to test drive cars until you know what features and styles you like because you'll commit to that choice for some time to come; typically, you'll drive the same car for many years!

While you won't wear your wedding dress more than once, you will look at the images for years to come. In either case, you won't know what you want until the search process is underway. If you are the type that sees it, likes it, and wraps it up, cherish the moment and enjoy the memorable journey.

For starters, you should choose a reputable, well-established retailer that shares your fashion style. Embrace the process and be open to expert guidance of a professional stylist assisting you on this special occasion.

Don't drive yourself crazy over the decision. Try not to obsess or become anxious. That's when you make a rushed, irrational choice that results in buyer's remorse. Take the pressure off, have fun, and enjoy the ride!

Chapter Four

How long are appointments? What do I need to bring to my appointment?

Brides often ask why we have a time limit to try gowns. This time limit could create pressure or anxiety at the idea of us keeping track of appointment time. On occasion, some brides feel the need to try an endless number of gowns and book two appointments with a different name. They'll then come into the store and tell us they want both time slots. We don't recommend doing this!

Needless to say, once they begin the process with the assigned Lovella stylist, they quickly realize the time allotted is more than sufficient in selecting the perfect wedding gown of choice.

At Lovella Bridal, we are your expert bridal fashion stylists. We guide each and every bride through a personalized strategic selection process to help find their dream gown. The key ingredient to our collective success in finding the perfect dress is our very unique process—the trust and deep sense of care we develop with one another.

If you're unable to shop at Lovella Bridal to find your perfect dress, this still applies to you regardless of where you're shopping: the longer you shop and the more gowns you see, the more overwhelmed you become. Seeing more gowns makes it more challenging to even remember what you have already tried.

Please note that it's not how many dresses you've randomly tried on; more importantly it's the number of dresses you've strategically tried on. Randomly trying an endless number of dresses distorts the pros and cons of your selection.

Strategic selection and the process of elimination helps narrow the field of possibilities, focusing on your overall vision, your story, and key elements of the gown that flatter your shape and suit your personality, enhancing your ability to make a sound decision with joy and celebration.

We typically give brides an hour to shop. Our philosophy is quality over quantity. With expert stylists on the job, we don't need more time because we've selected so strategically.

If I have a bride in the early stages of looking and feel she is not ready to finalize her decision, our major focus is to determine what she likes so we can narrow down styles.

After our appointment, we have a plan. Based on her progress, either she'll come back for a trunk show, or we book another appointment to see how she feels about the same gowns on a different day.

Sometimes life is just crazy. What happens if you book an appointment, the day arrives, and you just aren't feeling it? It's not about how long the appointment is in one sitting, especially if you're not having a productive session. Trying to prolong an ineffective session just wastes your time and elevates your anxiety.

You don't want to be in the store longer than an hour or an hour and a half. Otherwise, you'll become overwhelmed and struggle to figure out what direction you're going. Sometimes you need to walk away and come back in a week to revisit.

We'd rather you come back than have you try on dresses for four hours and be totally confused and walk out with nothing accomplished.

Chapter Five

Who should I bring with me to my appointment?

This choice is a personal one, but think long and hard about who you will include. This can make or break any shopping experience.

You want to bring those who understand and share your vision for your big day! If you don't have a vision yet, include those who know you best so they can help in the process of building your vision.

Let your guests know how you feel about pictures in advance to prevent unnecessary stress. We find that guests are so consumed with taking pictures that frankly they seem distracted and unable to fully engage in the experience. Pictures are a mixed blessing; they may offer some value but it may also be an obstacle by endlessly analyzing and dissecting. The best formula is to remain in the moment with optimum awareness, clarity, and feeling while in the dress looking at yourself.

For the majority of brides out there, there will most likely be certain guests you feel obligated to bring to your appointment. Perhaps it may be your aunt or mother-in-law to-be, whom you absolutely adore but know they don't share a similar vision of your attire on the day of your wedding. There are ways to include those you love without creating frustration for you or hurting their feelings.

I often recommend the bride invite friends and family members that know her best and fully support her vision for the wedding day.

If during the appointment, individuals who are influencing your decision-making process by projecting their own personal style and preferences over yours, it will lead to frustration and aggravation for you. Most importantly, it will create confusion.

Confusion begins when you start soliciting other people's opinions that are not aligned with your vision.

When someone says something to you, especially a person you value, that thought will remain in your head. For example: Countless brides buy gowns and come back to the store six months later to tell me they were pressured by their mom to buy a gown they didn't fully love.

"I bought it because my mom was in town and we felt pressured to have her with me when making the final decision. I ended up getting something because she loved it so much, but it isn't what I really wanted to wear for my wedding day."

Here we are, six months later, revamping a dress to make it suit the bride's wants and needs because she didn't have mental clarity to make her decision from the get go. She may also have felt obligated to listen to loved ones instead of her inner voice.

Many brides also have almost not purchased a dress they loved because a loved one made a comment like, "This dress looks like Christmas and you're getting married in summer." After that comment, the bride couldn't look at the dress they loved the way they did before.

Ladies, this is your decision. It is your gown. Your wedding. You must go with the gown that makes you look and feel the most beautiful, and be confident in that choice. Stay true to what you want and who you are. Loved ones will embrace and accept your selection despite the differences of opinion.

Every family and friend dynamic is different Coordinate appropriately to make this a positive experience for all involved.

Another option that may work for you is to first go through the process of making your dress selection alone or with loved ones that share your vision. Then invite individuals you wish to share the experience either prior to or soon after purchasing the dress. During this visit, know that the dress you selected may be criticized but welcomed because you love it.

Even though you've already made your selection, the purpose of this kind gesture is to embrace their participation with honor and respect. Another great option to consider is to plan to have your loved ones join the celebration with you when your dress arrives.

I also recommend pulling out what I like to call the "Bride's Secret." When you have loved ones pressuring you to include them in the shopping experience or who want to see the gown you've purchased, simply say, "I want it to be a surprise and would really love for everyone to see my dress for the first time when I walk down the aisle."

By showing everyone your dress, you rob them of that magical moment, seeing you for the first time on the day of your wedding. They already know what to expect. Shouldn't they have that first look with your fiancé and your entire wedding? Now that's just incredible!

When you show everyone what you will wear, the element of surprise will be gone. Feel free to pull out the "Bride's Secret" at any time. Works like a charm!

Chapter Six

Losing weight before trying on bridal gowns.

Looking your best on your wedding day is what we all want! So many of my brides tell me they have found their wonderful partner, and their favorite thing to do is to go out and spend time together. This often involves food.

Many who come in to try on gowns say they are having way too much fun exploring restaurants and have had little time to get into shape. The first thing they tell me is, "I promise I'm going to lose weight." For some people, this is true.

The biggest issue here is that brides often want to wait until they lose weight before they start the bridal gown shopping experience. This isn't a solid plan. If you wait to lose weight, you lose precious time when it comes to your gown being made. On average, most designers take six to eight months to manufacture a dress.

A lot can happen between that timeline with weight loss. If you wait too long, you won't have enough time to order a dress. You'll scramble at the last minute to find a manufacturer that can make a dress on time for you.

The best advice I can give you is to go shopping while feeling your worst with your weight. Embrace it.

You may think I'm totally crazy right now, but here's the deal: If you fall in love with a gown that you love on your body when you feel the most insecure about it, you will love it just the same whether you lose the weight or not.

Bottom line: Even when you lose the weight your proportions remain the same so what looks good on you today will look amazing on you the day of your wedding regardless if you lose the weight or not. The important message here is that you embrace and enjoy this process.

Just in case life does happen and you don't lose the weight, you still have a gown that you love. And that, my friends, is just priceless.

Now you may think, "Okay, fine. I don't agree with this, but I see your point. Let's say I go dress shopping, find a gown I love, and plan to lose thirty to fifty pounds. What size should I order?"

This is a valid question. Here's the deal: You have about six months to one year to figure out your body. A lot can change—or not change—during that time.

If you're determined to lose weight before you buy your gown, there are some things you must consider first.

You know your body and where you lose weight first. For instance, if you have wider hips as a result of your bone structure, you know the measurements there aren't going to change. In your bust and waist, however, you could possibly shed several inches.

In this case, you would order based on your hip measurement and plan to take in the rest after the dress is made.

This plan should work for any part of your body. If you know you're less likely to lose inches in your bust, but your posterior and waist are likely to drop a size or two, then plan around the bust and simply take in the other areas on the dress as you near the wedding date.

Another variable to consider is how you react to stress. Do you forget to eat or do you eat because that is the one thing gives you comfort? As your wedding date approaches, your stress levels are likely to increase.

Understanding your body's reaction to pressure can help you predict your weight loss abilities. Your expert stylist can guide you here.

Whatever you do, please don't wait to start shopping. Get in there and make sure you love how the gown looks on you the way you are and when you feel your worst. That is a guarantee for success.

Thousands of times, I've seen the joy when a bride comes in after she's lost her goal weight and the dress she loved when she didn't love her body surpasses what she anticipated it would look like.

Granted, she will swim in the fabric because the dress is too big, but what a great problem to have! Gowns can always be taken in, but they are very limited on how much can be let out.

Chapter Seven

I want to have my gown custom made.

The question I get asked weekly is, "I don't want to wear the same thing as anyone else. Do you suggest having a custom gown made?"

My answer, in every instance, is, "Absolutely not."

When it comes to your bridal gown, you will order your dress based on a store's sample. No matter which way you spin it, you won't really know how your completed dress will look until a month or so before your wedding.

Once it has been altered to your specifications or perhaps crafted in a different color from the sample you tried on, your dress could appear dramatically different than the exact same style ordered by another bride.

When you order a custom dress, you may also experience that uniqueness, but you'll also have no idea what it is going to look like, let alone how it will fit.

The biggest issue with custom ordering a gown is what the bride thought she would get and what the dressmaker created are two completely different things. There is no way for you or the dressmaker to concretely identify what the gown will look like if there is nothing to work off of.

In many cases, brides come into our store to purchase a sample a few months before their wedding because the gown they had made for them did not turn out how they envisioned.

These days, many designers no longer offer customizing. What you see is what you get. They do this because they don't want brides to be disappointed with what they buy.

One of the designers we feature in store is Berta Bridal. They don't even change the color of a gown. They make the sample in the color they feel looks best, and brides order everything as is.

These gowns retail above seven thousand dollars, and most brides who spend that amount expect custom sizing and changes.

But, guess what! Of all the past designs and designers that I've ever done custom changes, 99.9% of the time the bride isn't happy. So, while it may seem counterintuitive, it's actually ingenious that this company doesn't offer customization.

By not offering these custom changes, brides don't get tempted with all the possibilities. If they don't love all the elements about the dress they're considering, they just don't buy it. Then they're more likely to keep looking for a dress they do love.

The most common reasons for disappointment after gown customization include:

• When waiting six to eight months for your gown to arrive, a bride stares at the photo of the dress she tried on—without the custom changes she ordered. After all that staring, she begins to love the original design.

- What the bride envisioned the changes to look like and what she received are completely different.
- The final dress doesn't look like the sketch the designer provided. How can a drawing look like the finished product?

One thing a lot of designers do when designing lace gowns is put tulle fabric with a polka dot design (also called dotted swiss) underneath. The logic for this is that it fills in the empty areas where there is no lace, making the appearance and design more cohesive.

One bride asked if the dress could be ordered without the polka dot tulle layer, essentially leaving the areas with no lace completely empty. I asked the designer, and they approved the change.

When the dress came in, I was there working with the bride. We were both shocked by how different the dress looked. It really looked like a completely different dress.

Remember when I said above how a bride will look at the photo of herself in the sample gown she tried on for months and start to love it? Well, we thought the tulle removal was a simple change. The request cost extra, even with material being removed, because it was a custom order. She ended up hating the dress and was disappointed in the end.

The smartest thing you can do to prevent disappointment is minimize risk by not changing elements to an existing design. Your chances for disappointment grow exponentially when having a design created from scratch.

For the record, I have personally done many custom changes and had brides who were thrilled with the results, but it does take a certain type of individual. You need to have that appetite for risk and be okay with it not being exactly what you thought it would be.

One last item I'd like to touch on regarding choosing unique dresses is how many brides ask us to take the dress off the sales floor so their friends, family, or other women within their community can't purchase the same dress. This is a completely unrealistic request, of course.

However, if you feel that many people you know will purchase their dress from the same store you choose, and the other brides to-be won't tell you which dresses they have purchased, ask the store before shopping to look up which gowns a specific individual has purchased.

The store may not be able to tell you which dress was purchased, but with knowledge, they can steer you away from it.

Chapter Eight

What determines the cost of gowns? Buying a dress because it fits the budget!

When you first start shopping for gowns, it's difficult to know what they cost from looking at images. Prices are not usually listed online. Before booking an appointment, it's always a great idea to ask what their price range is for their inventory.

Bridal gown prices are determined by fabric quality, fit, construction, and cost of labor. By the looks of certain dresses, you may not be able to tell the price difference.

Once you start trying them on, you will feel and see the difference. For example, a lace dress can vary from $1,500 to $12,000 and more. This is simply because of the quality of the lace. Variations include imitation French lace from China or true French lace that comes from France, polyester versus silk, and cost of labor where the gown is being made.

We all have different ways of making decisions. It's important to think about this when setting a budget and when saying yes to the dress.

Whenever I have a bride that is indecisive, my first question is, "What is the primary driving factor to making your decision on your gown?" Most will tell me one of the following:

- What people think
- Cost
- How much I love it
- Fiancé's approval
- Parental approval

Once we are able to identify if this decision is driven by dollars or the emotional factor, that gives me clarity on what I need to focus on for my bride. Identifying how you are making this decision is important.

Your bridal gown is the most important article of clothing you'll ever wear, and it's a big deal. If you don't know what the driving factor of your decision making is, you will come to a place of indecision.

Indecision is usually code for "I don't have enough information to make a decision." Instead of focusing on how indecisive you are, you need to put that energy and attention toward making decisions. Be able to identify what matters most.

For example, about ten years ago, when I was a new bridal stylist, I had a bride tell me the most important thing for her wedding day was for her to find a gown she could visit the restroom in on her own. And I thought to myself "How the heck am I going to find something that fits her body, style, vision, and that she could use the bathroom on her own?"

At first I panicked because I had never had such a request, but after a moment, I was excited about the challenge. I found her the perfect Ines Di Santo dress that had an ultra-feminine Hollywood glam appearance that gave her the image she wanted for her big day. Best of all, she was able to move freely and use the restroom on her own.

The fact that this bride had identified the most important feature for her needs helped me in guiding her to make the right decision. Before you attend your appointment to try dresses on, I encourage you to think about the things you desire most out of your wedding day look. This may evolve and change as you search, but if you can, identify your ideal features from the beginning. This gives you and your stylist direction on your specific needs. If you don't have any, don't worry. We can figure it out.

This particular topic is important to me because I see people make the wrong decision all the time. Many times, brides find a gown they absolutely love that is beyond perfect for them, but they have difficulty justifying the cost.

In all the years I have been styling and dressing brides, I see them make the same mistake over and over and over again. I know using the word wrong is a bit strong, but it's true. It usually goes something like this: "I love this dress; it's my dress. It's over budget, but I can justify the cost."

Nayri K.

Scenario A:

A bride came in and loved a $12,000 dress from Lovella Bridal. She had a dressmaker elsewhere make it for her for $6,000. Four months before her wedding, she came back into the store to tell us she had decided to have the dress made and that it was the worst mistake.

She wanted to try on her favorite $12,000 dress again. Keep in mind that she had paid the dressmaker $4,000 that was non-refundable. She couldn't justify the $12,000 for the original dress she'd loved on top of what she'd already paid the dressmaker. Instead, she bought a $6,000 sample gown from our store, because at that point there was no time to order.

She came in again two months before her wedding and said she didn't love the sample dress she'd purchased. She tried on the $12,000 favorite again and then bought the sample of that one.

This individual ended up spending $22,000 instead of buying the $12,000 dress to begin with. This example may be dramatic, but it's a true story and this happens all the time.

The moral of the story is, even if a dress is over budget and you know it is your dress, rearrange your budget and make it fit from the beginning, instead of compromising and having to pay for it in the end financially or emotionally when you end up wearing a dress down the aisle that you don't even love.

Scenario B:

The bride came in for her alterations and purchased a dress that fit her $2,500 budget. The gown was absolutely gorgeous! During her shopping experience, she tried on dresses from other designers over her original set budget and fell in love with a $6,600 Edgardo Bonilla dress. Her fiancé couldn't justify the cost, so she bought the dress that fit her budget and not what she ultimately loved.

A week before the wedding, the bride was at her final fitting and said to her wedding fashion expert/stylist, "I should have listened to you and bought the dress I loved, even if it was over budget. Now I'm walking down the aisle in a gown I don't love, and it's too late to do anything about it."

These are just a couple of the most common examples I see over and over again. A bride fell in love with something over budget and ends up spending more than she would have had she just bought the original gown over budget.

The second most common example is when the bride picks the dress because someone else interfered with the decision-making process. She ultimately decides to go with a gown she doesn't really love because someone influenced her choice.

The worst part of all? Brides wear a dress down the aisle they don't love because it fit the budget. Breaks my heart every time! Consider going out for the night with friends and wearing an outfit you feel beautiful and confident in. You want to have that same feeling on your wedding day!

What you put on that morning is going to set the tone of your day, so you want to feel as confident and beautiful as possible. This is an area I would recommend not compromising on. You can't put a price on how you feel!

As a young adult, I worked so I could buy the things I wanted. I didn't have to rely on my parents to buy things for me or tell me why I could or couldn't have it. Once I was spending my own money that I worked so hard for, I had a hard time making decisions. I felt guilty if they told me certain things about what I bought.

I remember one day being so defeated because I bought an item that was a final sale, and my mom was angry that I chose that item to spend my hard-earned money on. But I really loved it. My dad said, "Enough! If you like it, you buy it!"

As simple as this sounds, it was a life-changer for me. For the first time, I realized I get to decide how I feel about something. I can choose to feel guilty or I can feel excited because I bought something that I like—even love—and I won't let anyone take that away from me.

If you like it, you buy it. End of story. And I'm sticking to it. There is nothing worse than wearing something down the aisle that you don't love.

Chapter Nine

I found the same gown I saw in store for thousands of dollars less online...

Counterfeit gowns have become an epidemic over the past six years in bridal, and in many other areas of formalwear fashion. Always remember that designer bridal gowns are not sold online. You must special order your gown through an authorized retailer listed on the designer's website.

Sometimes you may see the dress you saw in store in an image online, and the dress is listed for $300 to $500. This is fraud. Even if the actual designer is listed, don't fall for the scam.

We've worked with brides who ordered the gowns and didn't receive anything remotely close to the gown pictured. One bride I know got a lime green dress.

Do yourself a favor: Pick an authorized retailer with a good reputation, and support a local business that does the ethical thing.

Also, you may find stores that discount a designer gown. If they are legitimate and care about their contract with their designer, they are not allowed to discount products.

Think of it this way: If you were a designer and you had your collection represented in a store, would you want the store to devalue your product by lowering the price? I would assume not.

Most of us work hard for the money we earn. The last thing we'd want people to do is disrespect our hard, dedicated work. There is no point in price shopping.

Every legitimate retailer has to sell the same product for the same price. We don't make our own pricing; we aren't allowed to.

Regardless of the ways stores are willing to cut prices, the obvious reason is that the business is struggling. In a worst-case scenario, the store could be shut down before you receive your gown.

Alfred Angelo went out of business in 2017 and left thousands of brides across the nation without a dress. More importantly, the money they paid for the dress was gone.

I completely understand being on a budget and saving money, but at what cost? To what lengths are you willing to go to save a dime?

Chapter Ten

I'm not paying for the dress. How do I handle budgeting with who is paying?

Usually I like to recommend that you pay for your dress so you don't feel the stress of burdening someone else with the cost. However, if in some instances loved ones want to gift you your dress, have a conversation with that person so you're aware of what they are willing to spend.

For those who feel like they need to convince a loved one on the cost of your gown, here's how I advise you to go about it. This historically works well.

Let's say, for example, that you're going to ask your fiancé for the funds to purchase the gown.

You can apply this to anyone who might pay, but for simplicity, we'll use fiancé for these scenarios.

Scenario 1:

"I went bridal gown shopping today and found a dress I absolutely love. I would love to get it, but I know it's more than what we discussed. If that isn't okay with you, I'll try to find a similar one that costs less."

Scenario 2:

"I went bridal gown shopping today and found the gown of my dreams! I can't imagine wearing anything else to get married in; it's just perfect. Everything I've ever wanted and more. Makes me even more excited to get married. I just can't wait to walk down the aisle to marry the love of my life!"

If you were the fiancé, or any other loved one who'd offered to purchase the dress, which scenario would you say yes to? Point made!

If you love something, go for it! You know how I feel about purchasing something you love, especially your bridal gown. In life, we compromise on many things.

However, your bridal gown is the one thing you just don't want to compromise on. You deserve to wear whatever makes you feel beautiful and excited to marry the love of your life. No one is going to fight for that but you!

Chapter Eleven

What is a trunk show versus a sample sale?

Trunk shows and sample sales are often believed to be the same exact thing. It's not unusual to confuse the two. Here's why:

It's impossible for a store to feature every gown from each designer they represent. Trunk show weekends give brides the opportunity to shop a wider selection from a specific designer than what the store typically has in stock. Trunk shows are also a way to see the latest and greatest designs that are not yet available in stores.

Trunk shows occur when one particular designer brings in a larger gown selection from their collection to the store for a short period of time. The trunk shows typically last three days: Friday, Saturday, and Sunday.

As an additional bonus, trunk shows also give brides a chance to access the latest styles with enough time to place an order. Just like it takes a bride approximately six to eight months to receive her dress, that's also how long it takes for bridal stores to receive their stock or sample gowns.

Brides to-be see the latest and greatest designs online as soon as they debut on the runway and can't wait six to eight months before trying on. Trunk shows give designers the opportunity to debut their latest designs not yet available in stores for brides to pre-purchase straight from the runway at a trunk show.

Depending on the store and designer, there may also be special pricing or incentives during the trunk show. It is not a deep discount like you would receive during a sample sale, but we'll cover that in just a moment.

We recommend that you explore the store's selection and designers before attending a specific trunk show. You will likely find that you gravitate to particular designers—maybe even just one designer. Only attend the trunk show after you've already shopped that particular designer in store.

Shopping the store prior to the trunk show takes off the pressure of feeling like you haven't seen enough dresses. When you have already determined which designer you want to wear and want to see more designs to make your final selection, then you should visit a trunk show.

Trunk shows are a buying experience. The gowns visiting the store that weekend are only available for purchase that weekend. By shopping the store first, you won't feel the pressure to make a choice on the spot if you don't feel prepared. You can revisit your favorites in store along with the new designs and feel super confident in your final choice.

On many occasions, brides will buy at the trunk show even though it is their first time shopping. However, these brides may have already had their eye on that designer and don't want to wear any other label. Other times, they stumble upon a gem and are so confident, they go for it. If you want to explore, we do not suggest doing so at a trunk show. Leave those appointments for brides interested in that designer as the time these gowns are available in store is limited to the weekend.

Now, let's discuss sample sales. Sample sales are when stores sell the physical samples brides try on when shopping for a dress. On occasion, floor models (also known as samples) go on sale to make room for new inventory coming in. Sometimes the gown has been discontinued and is no longer being manufactured by the designer.

Many don't realize gowns can be discontinued at any time. You may fall in love with a gown and decide to wait a few weeks or months to purchase, only to realize it is no longer available for special order. The store can't predict this, and there is no way to give a bride prior notice.

Sample sales are perfect for a bride on a budget, a bargain hunter, or someone that does not have enough time to order and alter a dress. You'll save money and have the dress immediately.

When shopping sample sales, you'll want to know what sizes the gowns are that you'll be shopping.

Be realistic of what is possible to alter and what isn't. If the dress is slightly small, you can make it work by having a seamstress do a corset lace-up back instead of the zipper. That always works well.

All sample gowns large or snug on your body can be altered to some degree, but be realistic in your expectations of the sizing or modifications and asses each gown situation accordingly. Bridal gowns, in general, run small compared to regular dress sizes. A gown being considered too big to alter is subject to the opinion of your seamstress.

For easy reference, sample gowns are often the middle of the size chart, or bridal size ten to twelve (subject to differ; consult your local bridal store).

There are some important things to know when buying a sample. Be realistic on the condition of the dress. Don't drive yourself, loved ones, or the seamstress crazy with every little detail being perfect. It is a sample and will never look brand new. There may be little imperfections here and there that only you would know, and that's why you got a great deal on it.

Brides often want to dry clean the dress before wearing it. This could turn out to be a huge mistake. For starters, there is always the possibility of potential damage through the dry cleaning process. It's a mechanical and chemical process; things can happen.

This cleaning process may also possibly dull the fabric or damage embellishment, if any. It's perfectly fine to dry clean and preserve your gown after the wedding, but you don't want any surprises before your big day.

However, if dry cleaning before wearing it down the aisle is necessary, be sure to select a dry cleaner with expertise in bridal gown cleaning and preservation.

Chapter Twelve

What are sample gown sizes?

The majority of bridal stores carry sample gowns in bridal size ten and twelve, which is about a six or an eight in American street clothing sizing. These sizes are in the middle of the size chart.

Just as bridal gowns have long lead times for brides, the same is true for a bridal store with their stock order.

Many designers only give bridal stores the option to order a ten or twelve in bridal gowns because they can produce the same two sizes faster than filling a bunch of different size orders. This allows stores to get the inventory in store sooner but can be challenging for the opposite ends of the spectrum on the size chart.

If you are a size zero or two, you'll swim in the fabric and it can be difficult to see what the proportions of the gown will look like in your size. If you are a size fourteen or higher, you won't be able to get the dresses on.

This is a challenge many women experience when bridal gown shopping. It is unfortunate, but this is how the bridal industry is structured. It's simply too expensive for stores to order multiple sizes and, as stated above, if we did order multiple sizes, they would take forever to arrive to the store.

You will want to contact your local bridal store to see what sample sizes they offer. Some stores, including Lovella, have also expanded to feature sample size gowns size fourteen and up.

Keep in mind each designer's size chart varies; you will not be the same size in every designer. Sizing is determined by your bust, waist, and hip measurements.

Choose the size that most closely matches your measurements. If for example, your hips are your largest part, you will need to order a gown to accommodate your hips and take in the waist and bust.

No bridal gown arrives fitting perfectly. You will always need alterations. Bridal gowns have fit and structure unlike any other article of clothing you'll wear, which is why alterations play such a vital role in this process.

Chapter Thirteen

What to expect during the alteration process.

When you think of fashion today, most materials we wear have some sort of stretch or give to them. Designers opt for more forgiving materials and shapes, which means we've all gotten used to feeling really comfortable in our daily attire.

This also means many of us don't typically get clothing altered. When we do, it's something small like shortening a pant or sleeve—in my case, lengthening sleeves.

Your bridal gown alteration process will be unlike any other alteration you've experienced. The majority of bridal gowns have a lot of structure and many layers of materials that everyday clothing does not.

Bridal gown alterations are not something every seamstress is capable of undertaking. Altering a wedding gown requires a specialized level of expertise to ensure the best possible fit given the unique elements of the gown and body type.

The specialty of creating the perfect fit is truly an art form. The artistic knowledge coupled with technical capabilities are key components in ensuring impeccable fit while upholding the aesthetic look and design of the gown.

When ordering your bridal gown, your size is determined by your bust, waist, and hip measurements, taking into consideration the most dominant measurement.

Every body is uniquely created with defined proportions. Our goal is to order the size that will allow for proper alterations to achieve the best possible fit without limitations.

You may have heard comments like, "It's better to take in than to let it out." If your hips or bust are your most dominant measurements, we will recommend ordering a size that fits these measurements, even if it's larger than you expect.

This enables the seamstress to sculpt the gown to your body with the comfort of knowing we have options. Even if you order a dress that is custom-sized to your measurements or a size well within the selected designer size chart, there is still a good possibility it will not fit you perfectly. It may need to be adjusted once on your body.

You can expect most bridal gowns will require body work (taking in the body or letting out if too snug), hemming (shortening the gown), and a bustle (gathering the train up during reception).

The alteration process is the most important step to making sure your dress fits just right! We see gowns transform in front of our eyes on a daily basis.

Chapter Fourteen

Why are alterations so expensive?

When you budget for your bridal gown, it is important to include the alteration cost. When doing research on what bridal stores you plan to visit, ask them the average price of alterations so you are aware before setting a budget for your gown.

Have you ever heard the sayings, "You get what you pay for," and, "If it sounds too good to be true, it probably is"?

Well, I live by these two quotes, because I have lived through situations that have taught me these hard lessons.

I'll never forget the one experience that really drove home, "If it sounds too good to be true, it probably is."

I had recently moved home from college. I started working in bridal retail full time and became obsessed with all elements of fashion. I read books on Hermès and the Birkin bag and became fixated on owning a Birkin, given the history of fashion and what the Birkin represents. I just loved the history behind this bag and the story of it.

Sidenote: My mom has called me the bag lady since I was about ten years old. She still doesn't know where I get it, because she has carried the same handbag since I was a kid. She just keeps buying new ones of the same thing to replace the old.

Anyway, I found a Craigslist ad for a coveted crocodile Birkin bag. I studied everything I possibly could to determine if this bag was real or fake. The second I saw it up close, I knew it was fake and the ad was a total lie.

I didn't buy it, but I thought, "Gosh darn it. 'If it sounds too good to be true, it sure is!'" I promised myself I would never try to buy a luxury item for a fraction of the cost ever again, because it couldn't possibly be realistic. I was twenty-two when this happened, and I'm thankful now for this experience.

This applies to not only fashion-related things, but also to anything in life. If you want the real deal, you have to work for it and do it the right way.

For quality work, you have to pay. There is just no way around it. I have watched countless seamstresses labor away, hour after hour, on these bridal gowns, and the amount of talent, artistry, patience, and love for their craft is unparalleled.

Without this step, your bridal gown will not be what it should be on the day of your wedding. If it is not altered properly, it doesn't matter which designer you wear. It's all about the fit. This is the final piece of the puzzle and the most important one.

Your bridal gown will be the most expensive article of clothing you will ever have altered. The reason for this is because when you look at fashion today, most of the clothes we wear will stretch and form to our bodies so we don't have to alter them.

A bridal gown has structure and a fit unlike anything you've ever worn and requires a certain level of attention to fit your body properly.

Do not discount the importance of finding a store and seamstress that knows what they are doing. If a store offers you free alterations, run!

The amount of talent and expertise required for this kind of job is costly. It's an art form, and no person will work for free because they can't, and frankly it just isn't right. We all deserve to be compensated for our work.

We, like many stores, have had brides decide our alterations are too expensive, usually because a family member told them so. They take their gown elsewhere for alterations to be done. Shortly after taking the gown, they call us after the fact and ask if we can fix the mishaps.

One bride called and said, "The seamstress I took my dress to cut my train off. Can you reattach it for me?"

There is a huge difference between an average tailor versus an expert bridal gown seamstress. There are so many stories like this.

Even in our own alteration department, things may happen. The difference is, we work with bridal gowns all day long. We are solution-oriented to make sure we have exhausted all possibilities to have gowns fit the bride as comfortably and as beautifully as possible.

You could experience possible malfunctions on the day of the wedding. Some of the most common include:

- Zipper broke
- Hook and eye popped off
- The dress was too long and was tripped on all night
- Bustle busted/ripped off
- Dress was too tight
- Dress was falling off
- Strap broke

The list above contains just a few examples of things we hear that are most common the day of the wedding. You must know that your gown is an article of clothing and will stretch, just like a pair of jeans. It's impossible to predict how a gown will behave on your body the day of your wedding, and that is not the designer's fault nor the alterations' fault. These are things that happen that we are unable to predict; it's part of life.

Once, I was getting into a cab to the Ines Di Santo runway show during New York bridal fashion week. As I lifted my leg, the entire seam down the back of my dress came undone. It literally snapped, and my booty was out for New York City to see. I couldn't blame the store or designer for that happening. I moved my leg a certain way, and that was all it took for the thread to snap.

You must be aware of these possibilities, and be ready to tackle any of the above, as well as anything else you haven't yet considered. Malfunctions like these are so common for the bride, bridal party, and anyone else involved in the wedding.

Some companies offer services the day of the wedding that specialize in repairing malfunctions and know how to properly get you in and out of your dress.

This is a great resource to have on your wedding day in case you or your guests need a quick repair to make the night as magical as possible.

One day, during an alteration appointment, my bride's mom said, "Honey, things are going to go wrong on the wedding day. I want you to not care about them so you can enjoy the day, because you have a choice. You can focus on the bad or the good, and honey, I promise you there will be more good than bad that day. I want your focus to be on the good."

I thought, "Wow, what an awesome mom!" By mentally preparing her daughter for things to go wrong—because let's face it, this isn't about being negative; it's about being real—she preemptively took some of the stress away. Does anything go 100% according to plan? No! But somehow, some way, it always works itself out.

I just loved this, because it set the bride up to truly enjoy and make the most out of her wedding day. She could live in the moment, no matter what may go wrong.

If you want to be as stress-free as possible, think of all the negative possible outcomes and have solutions ready for those things. Hire an onsite dresser and repairer the day of for any outfit malfunction the bridal party and groomsmen may experience. At the very least, have a day-of-event coordinator.

Chapter Fifteen

I bought a dress I thought I loved and now I'm not so sure.

I tell every bride who purchases her gown from me to leave her decision in the store. What do I mean by that? Well, what other item do you purchase by placing an order and then waiting months for that item?

Special-order items always take time to deliver, giving you too many chances between purchase and receipt to question your choice.

When you leave the store after you've completed the purchase, you may no longer feel the emotional connection you felt when you looked at yourself in the mirror.

The only way to keep even a hint of that connection is to remember the feeling. Remember your own reflection. Don't go home and look at the photos and analyze the decision. By staring at the photo, you replace those memories by analyzing every detail, which leads to questioning your decision.

If you feel remotely nervous after purchasing your dress, you can always ask to go back in store and try it on again in person to reassure yourself you made the right choice. When it comes to your bridal gown, you make the decision when you are in the dress, not by looking and a photo or sleeping on it.

It's a feeling. A feeling of beauty, excitement, and confidence that can only happen when you are in it!

If you have a need to analyze the gown, do so before you purchase. After you have finalized your decision, leave your decision in the bridal store and move on to another element of planning your wedding.

Chapter Sixteen

Am I supposed to feel the magic brides talk about?

My favorite part in an appointment when working with a bride is the moment they turn around ask with a worried expression, "Am I supposed to just feel it? How do I know it's the one? I'm not feeling anything."

Buying a wedding dress is similar to buying a car. You will explore all the features and elements you like until you find one that fits all your wants and needs—the one that makes you smile and get excited when you see it.

If you're the type to cry when exciting things happen in your life, you might even shed some tears. If you're not the type of person that gets overly excited about these types of things—if you're logical and make rational decisions with all information given—you may not cry or feel the "magic."

Many brides ask how they could possibly pick a dress because they like so many of them. This happens all the time at Lovella Bridal because we have such a remarkable selection.

With over 6,000 square feet of space, we definitely have the room to store them. It's common for a bride to find many dresses that she likes. Trust me; you will know when it is the one.

Even if you like two dresses and are having a hard time deciding, there will be certain features that make the choice for you. Try them both on back-to-back and keep going back and forth between the two. Then choose the dress that makes you feel the most excited to put on—the one that makes you light up just a bit more.

Your wedding dress sets the tone for how you feel the day of your wedding. Pick the one that, as soon as the zipper zips, you get excited and feel absolutely beautiful and wifey ready!

End Notes

It's been an absolute pleasure taking you on this journey through bridal fashion and showing you a bit of my world!

I sincerely hope for this book to become a segue for you to better understand the industry, and most of all, to enable you to make favorable choices and enhance your bridal gown shopping experience.

My last word of advice: Enjoy every moment! Your wedding day comes and goes so quickly. You spend all this time planning and stressing over every detail. When the wedding day arrives, let everything go and ENJOY!

I'm getting married...

Who cares if something goes wrong? The day passes faster than you can ever imagine, so soak it all up and celebrate!

It has been my absolute honor to be a part of your wedding experience. Wishing you and your life partner an abundance of love and joy!

All the best,

Nayri

Acknowledgements

To my mother, who has always supported my vision and life goals 1,000% and been right by my side every step of the way! Thank you for trusting in me and always encouraging me to do bigger and better. To my dad, for always believing in me, even when my ideas seem so outrageous, he doesn't know what to say and just gives a huge smile of approval because he knows I can! I'm thrilled I was chosen to be your daughter!

To my brother, the first person to hear about this book and tell me how I must do it! You're always pushing me out of my comfort zone, since before I could even walk or talk.

To my grandparents: Thank you for all you sacrificed, leaving everything you knew to come to America to live the American dream. None of this would be possible without your tireless determination and boldness to leave loved ones behind for new opportunity. Thank you!

To my extended family—aunts, uncles and cousins—who really are not so extended, as I consider them all immediate family: I love you all! Your endless love and support for anything I do is unparalleled. You are my number one fans, and I appreciate each and every one of you more than you know!

Rozi, our head seamstress at Lovella Bridal, you watched me evolve from the beginning of time. Thank you for all that you do and for your constant words of encouragement. With your ingenious expertise and guidance to me personally and our entire alteration team, our Lovella Brides walk down the aisle with confidence.

Kristina, I am grateful that I was home from college and working in 2009 during break to do your alteration appointment! We've been together ever since. Wouldn't have wanted to share this journey with anyone else. Can't imagine living this life without you.

Laura, I was overjoyed when my dad found you and led you to Lovella! You are one of a kind and your endless support, love, and kindness is my continued motivation.

To my Lovella Bridal Family—wedding fashion experts, stylists, and seamstresses: This book is for each and every one of you! Blessed to have you all in my life! We have the most magical job in the entire world, touching women's hearts daily and making forever memories with them. We help them find the most important article of clothing they will ever wear. I wouldn't want to do that job without any of you!

To my coaches and mentors: Thank you for believing in me and encouraging me. I am forever grateful for your guidance and wisdom!

About the Author

Born and raised in Los Angeles, Nayri grew up amid the high-fashion bridal industry, knowing that one day she, too, would join that realm of fashion. Nayri has been a part of the Lovella Family for over ten years and is one of three buyers behind Lovella's inventory.

"My favorite element of what I do for a living is that it doesn't feel like work – I am here each day to serve our brides and to assist women in feeling the most beautiful and confident on one of the most important days in their life. That is just priceless!"

At age eight or ten, she would stand in front of a huge mirror in her parents' bedroom and design bridal and evening gowns from bath towels. She especially loved walking down the stairs and watching the bath towel train trail behind her.

Photo Credit: Starla Fortunato
Gown Credit: Ines Di Santo

Another favorite would be to dress up in her mom's work clothes and pretend she was going to work with her briefcase.

She loves to work and loves fashion... NOTHING has changed. She was literally born to do what she's doing today.

Stay in touch with Nayri by subscribing to her YouTube channel and podcast on iTunes to access ever-evolving tips:

Website:
www.weddingfashionexpert.com

YouTube:
YouTube.com/WeddingFashionExpert

Instagram:
instagram.com/weddingfashionexpert

Facebook:
facebook.com/WeddingFashionExpert

About Lovella Bridal

Lovella Bridal is an industry trendsetter making bridal gown dreams come true for over 46 years. Since 1970, our Lovella buyers have been continuously searching the world to ensure Lovella's collections are unique, relevant, and aligned with the individual tastes and high standards of our discerning clients.

Lovella Bridal expanded to a beautiful store front of over 6,000 square feet of space across from The Americana at Brand in Glendale in 2013. Since this move and expansion, our primary focus has always been to have the best service, quality inventory, and selection in the greater Los Angeles area.

Not only do we strive to be the front runner in our industry, we also aim to have a variety of price points with bridal gowns starting at $2,000, never compromising on quality.

This is why we are known for our exceptional service, knowledge, inventory, and beautiful store.

Photo Credit: Starla Fortunato
Gown Credit: Edgardo Bonilla
Accessories: Maria Elena Headpieces

We are most proud of our brides. Everything our Lovella Family does is in the best interest of our brides, and we are SO proud of being a part of such a memorable day.

Making women feel confident and beautiful and watching them grow their families—it is the most rewarding thing to witness, and that our hard work brings women joy and love for generations to come.

What sets us apart is our unparalleled service and the knowledge our bridal stylists have. We are the bridal store you visit to meet YOUR personal shopper and stylist for your wedding day!

We invite you to personally visit our custom designed store for a once in a lifetime experience in selecting your bridal gown!

Visit us at www.lovellabridal.com to book your appointment today.

Pricing:

Opening price point for bridal gowns in store: $2,000.

Contact Info:

Lovella Bridal
Address: 224 South Brand Boulevard
Glendale, CA 91204
Website: www.lovellabridal.com
Phone: 818-246-4637
Email: info@lovellabridal.com

Instagram:
instagram.com/lovellabridal
instagram.com/lovellaplus

Facebook:
facebook.com/LovellaBrides
facebook.com/LovellaPlus

Glossary

Common Terms Used
During Bridal Gown Shopping

Train

Train refers to the longest part of the skirt trailing behind the bride. Because trains vary in length, the following terms best describe size of train from shortest to longest: sweep, chapel, cathedral. Trains can often be extended or shortened so go with a train length that suits you.

I advise brides not to get caught up on the terms because nowadays designers create their own train length and don't necessarily abide by the three categories listed.

Bustle

The bustle refers to lifting up and securing the longest part of the train. The bustle is created by the seamstress during your fitting.

Wearing a bridal gown with a train trailing behind you as you walk down the aisle is one of the exciting and dramatic elements of wearing a wedding dress, but how are you supposed to dance the night away with all that fabric? This is why you need a bustle. Regardless of length or shape of train, almost all dresses can be bustled.

It is important to have your shoes during the alteration process to determine the length of gown in front and back. Customarily the bustle is slightly longer than the front of your dress.

Hem

Hemming a gown refers to shortening the length of the dress primarily in front offering mobility and functionality.

Bridal gowns come in a standard length. If you're extremely tall you may need to order extra length. Most brides will require shortening of the hem because the standard length is too long.

Occasionally some gowns may be the perfect length, where hemming is not required. This is extremely rare but also possible.

Veil

Veil refers to the tulle that brides wear in their hair while walking down the aisle.

Veils are typically made of tulle attached to a comb. They come in various shapes and sizes. Some veils are plain, have lace, embroidery, embellishment, etc.

Veils are the icing on the cake for your bridal gown! They have been worn for centuries and are an iconic tradition.

Blusher

Similar to a veil, the blusher is a shorter version—generally 30 to 45 inches in length—attached to a comb. Sometimes a blusher may be attached to the veil on one comb.

Traditionally brides wear short tulle veils to drape over their face during the ceremony. This is purely based on personal preference.

Notes

Notes

Made in the USA
Las Vegas, NV
02 September 2022

54599405R00075